GRANDPARENTS

of the

BIBLE

by

ELMER TOWNS

Grandfather of 10 — Great Grandfather of 6

DESTINY IMAGE® PUBLISHERS, INC.

P.O. Box 310, Shippensburg, PA 17257-0310

"Promoting Inspired Lives."

This book and all other Destiny Image and Destiny Image Fiction books are available at Christian bookstores and distributors worldwide.

For more information on foreign distributors, call 717-532-3040.

Or reach us on the Internet: www.destinyimage.com

ISBN 13 978-0-7684-1433-2

For Worldwide Distribution, Printed in the U.S.A.

1 2 3 4 5 6 7 8 9 10 11 /17 16 15 14

Content

Jacob

The Spiritual Giver

A. INTRODUCTION: GENESIS 48:1-22

1. What can a "_____"
   grandfather give to a son who has everything?

2. What can an _____
   grandfather give to children he seldom sees?

3. What can a _____ grandfather
   give to his grandchildren?

4. What can a grandfather give, who has _____
   to give?

B. FOUR THINGS GRANDFATHER SAID TO THEM

1. Jacob told them _____
   . *"God Almighty appeared to me at Luz in the land of
   Canaan"*(v.3). Was this Jacob's salvation experience?
   "The angel, which redeemed me from evil" (v.16).

WHAT'S INVOLVED IN A TESTIMONY?

What you _____ before salvation.

What you did to _____ .

How you were _____ .

"God before whom my fathers, Abraham, and Isaac did walk, the God which fed me all my life long until this day" (v.15).

1. Jacob told them the _____.
    He told them God's _____,
    God's _____ and God's _____
    (vv.15-17).

2. Jacob told them the four-fold promise of God (v.4).

    a. _____. *"Behold I will make thee fruitful."*

    b. _____. *"I will multiply thee."*

    c. _____. *"I will make of thee a multitude of people."*

    d. _____. I will give this land to thy seed after thee for an everlasting possession."

OMITTED FROM ABRAHAM'S COVENANT

Bless these who bless you.
Curse your enemies.
Make name great.

5   Jacob told them about their _____.
     *"When I came from Padan, Rachel died by me in the
     land of Canaan in the way, when yet there was a little
     way to come to Ephrath, and I buried her there"* (v.7).

6.   Your grandmother died in _____.

     a.   I _____ when she died.

     b.   We were _____.

     c.   She was buried by the _____.

C. FOUR THINGS GRANDFATHER DID FOR THEM

1.   Jacob _____ them. *"Now these
     two sons, Ephraim and Manasseh...are mine"* (v.5). The
     boys were half Hebrew and half Egyptian.

2.   Jacob _____ them.
     *Jacob showed his affection. 'He kissed them and em-
     braced them"* (v.10).

3.   Jacob laid _____. *"And Israel
     stretched out his right hand, and laid it upon Ephraim's
     head, who was the younger, and his left hand up-
     on Manasseh's head, guiding his hands wittingly; for
     Manasseh was the firstborn"* (v.14). The word *wittingly*
     means Jacob knew what he was doing.

4.   Jacob _____ his grandchildren.
     *"By faith Jacob when he was dying, blessed both the sons
     of Joseph"* (Heb. 11:21).

How to Bless Children

Step 1:   A meaningful touch.

Step 2:   Blessing with a spoken word.

Step 3:   Attach high value to the one being blessed.

Step 4:   Picture a special future for the one being blessed.

Step 5:   An active commitment to fulfilling the blessing.

—From *God Bless You*, by Elmer Towns

D. FOUR THINGS GRANDFATHER GAVE THEM

1. Jacob gave them _____. Jacob adopted the two boys. "They are mine" (v.5). "Let my name be upon them, and the name of my father Abraham and Isaac" (v.16).

2. Jacob gave _____ to them. *"Let them grow into a multitude in the midst of the earth"* (v.16). *"And he blessed them that day, saying, in thee shall Israel bless, saying, God make thee as Ephraim and as Manasseh; and he set Ephraim before Manasseh"* (v. 20).

3. Jacob gave them _____.

4. Jacob gave them an _____.

    a. The _____ of worship. "He (Jacob) bowed himself with his face to the earth" (v.12).

    b. The _____ of worship. "Jacob...worshipped, leaning upon the top of his staff" (Heb. 11:21).

E. FOUR LESSONS TO TAKE AWAY

1. Grandparents should be concerned about the _____ of their grandchildren.

2. Grandparents shall be a _____.

3. Grandparents should give their _____.

4. Grandparents should bless (_____ and spiritually).

Naomi

A Compromising Mother Becomes a Godly Grandmother

A. HOW NAOMI COMPROMISED

1. She compromised her _____.

    a. Did not continue in difficulties. "A famine in the land" (Ruth 1:1).

    b. Enticed by the well-watered plains of Moab (1:1).

    c. Left the Promised Land. *"Ephrathites of Bethlehem, Judah"* (1:2).

2. She compromised her commitment _____.
    When Ruth, her daughter-in-law wanted to go with Naomi, she directed her to go back to her foreign god. *"Look, your sister-in-law has gone back to her people and to her gods; return after your sister-in-law"* (1:15).

3. Naomi compromised her _____.
    Naomi's son, Chilion, married outside the faith (1:4).

4. Naomi _____ God's provision for her. *"I went out full, and the Lord has brought me home again empty"* (1:21).

B. NAOMI'S REPENTANCE
SEEN IN HER ACTIONS

1. _____. Naomi recognized God's
   punishment. *"The Lord hath caused me to suffer, and
   the Almighty has sent me such tragedy"* (1:21, NLB).

2. _____. When Ruth "happened"
   on Boaz's field, Naomi said, *"Blessed be he of the Lord,
   who has not forsaken His kindness to the living and the
   dead! And Naomi said to her, This man is a relation of
   ours, one of our close relatives"* (2:20).

3. Naomi counseled toward _____.
   *"Then Naomi her mother-in- law said unto her, 'My
   daughter, shall I not seek security for you, that it may be
   well with you?'"* (3:1).

4. Naomi counseled _____.
   *"Then she (Naomi) said, 'Sit still, my daughter...for the
   man will not rest until he has concluded the matter this
   day'"* (3:18).

C. THE BLESSING ON
GRANDMOTHER NAOMI

*"Then the women said to Naomi, 'Blessed be the Lord,
who has not left you this day without a close relative;
and may his name be famous in Israel! And may he be
to you a restorer of life and a nourisher of your old age;
for your daughter-in-law, who loves you, who is better
to you than seven sons, has borne him'"* (Ruth 4:14-15).

1. Naomi is given _____ in the Bible than Ruth.

   a. The women blessed Naomi (4:14).

   b. The child is recognized as "kin" to Naomi (4:14).

   c. Naomi had oversight for the child's care (4:16).

2. The child is _____ with this grandmother (not father or grandfather). Note: legal line not through Naomi and Elimelach (4:21).

3. The child Obed would be _____.

   a. The word famous means, "name is proclaimed widely."

   b. Obed was the _____ of Daniel.

   c. Obed comes from two words, (1) *Obadiah* i.e., a _____ _____, (2) *ebed*, i.e., _____. Obed was a true servant and worshipper of the Lord.

4. The child gave grandmother Naomi a _____.

   a. Naomi had been a _____, but she became a woman of _____.

   b. Naomi didn't have _____. She told Ruth, *"Turn back, my daughters, go-for I am too old to have a husband. If I should say I have hope, if I should have a husband tonight and should also bear sons"* (1:12). But God gave her a _____. *"He (Obed) shall be unto thee, a restorer of life"* (4:15).

    c. Naomi had no _____. *"Call me Mara, for the Almighty hath dealt very bitterly with me" (1:20)*. But Obed _____ her old age. *"And may he (Obed) be to you a restorer of life and a nourisher of your old age"* (4:15).

5. Naomi gained _____ of her daughter-in-law. *"Then the women said to Naomi, 'Blessed be the Lord...your daughter-in-law, who loves you, who is better to you than seven sons"* (4:14-15).

6. Naomi had the responsibility of _____ the child.

    a. Naomi was given a _____ to rear a son.

    b. A rich man like Boaz would have _____ for children, i.e., he got Naomi.

    c. *"Then Naomi took the child and laid him on her bosom, and became a nurse to him"* (4:16).

Asa

A Revival Grandson Came from an Ungodly Grandmother

"In the twentieth year of Jeroboam king of Israel, Asa became king over Judah. And he reigned forty-one years in Jerusalem. His grandmother's name was Maachah the granddaughter of Absalom. Asa did what was right in the eyes of the Lord, as did his father David. And he banished the perverted persons from the land, and removed all the idols that his fathers had made. Also he removed Maachah his grandmother from being queen mother, because she had made an obscene image of Asherah. And Asa cut down her obscene image and burned it by the brook Kidron" (I Kings 15:9-13).

A. MAACHAH: AN UNGODLY GRANDMOTHER

1. _____. Her name Maachah means "fighting" or "oppression."

2. _____. Maachah was rebellious like her grandfather Absalom. *"His (Abijam) mother's name was Maachah, the daughter of Absalom (Absalom)"* (1 Kings 15:2).

    a. Absalom _____ his brother
Amnon. *"Absalom had commanded…when I say
strike Amnon, then kill him"* (II Sam. 13:28).

    b. Absalom pretended to be loyal to his father David.
"So Absalom stole the hearts of the men of Israel"
(II Sam. 15:6).

    c. Absalom tried to _____ his father
David. *"Make haste to depart from the city of David
lest he overtake us suddenly…and strike the city with
the edge of the sword"* (II Sam. 15:14).

3. Grandmother Maachah influenced her husband
Rehoboam to _____.

    a. *"Rehoboam loved Maachah the daughter of Absalom
more than all his wives and his concubines…and
Rehoboam made Abijah the son of Maachah as chief
to be leader over his brethren, for he intended to
make him King"* (II Chron. 11:20-22).

    b. Rehoboam's sin _____ the kingdom.

    c. Rehoboam's continuing sin _____
the kingdom. *"And he (Rehoboam) did evil because
he did not prepare his heart to seek the Lord"*
(II Chron. 12:14).

4. Grandmother Maachah gave her son
an _____. The son of Maachah was
Abijah (II Chron. 12:16 ff) whose name means, "The
Lord is my Father," but the boy also was given the
name *Abijam*, which means "My father is Yam" a
Canaanite God of the sea.

5. Maachah supported sexual _____.
"And Asa took away all the sodomites out of the land,

*and removed all the (filthy) idols that his father (Abijam)
had made"* (I Kings 15:12).

6. Maachah worshipped _____.
   *"Asa removed all the idols that his father and mother had
   made"* (I Kings 15:12-13, ELT).

7. Maachah secretly had a _____ goddess-idol.
   She had made an obscene image to Asherah. *"And Asa
   cut down her obscene idol and burned it by the brook
   Kidron"* (I Kings 15:13).

   a. Idols usually represent a _____.

   b. Maachah was utterly _____.

B. ASA, A GODLY GRANDSON

1. Asa reacted to the _____ of his father.
   *"Abijam walked in all the sins of his father which he had
   done before him (evil example), and his heart was not
   perfect with the Lord his God, or the heart of David"*
   (I Kings 15:3-4). The principle: extreme abuses lead to
   reformation.

2. God _____ Asa to carry on the
   godly rule of David. *"Nevertheless for David's sake did
   the Lord his God give him a lamp in Jerusalem to set
   up his son (Asa) after him, and to establish Jerusalem"*
   (I Kings 15:4).

3. Asa began with reforms (II Chronicles 14:2-7).

   a. Repented of _____. *"He (Asa)
      removed the altars of the foreign gods and the high*

places, and broke down the sacred pillars and cut down the wooden images" (II Chron. 14:3).

b. Commanded the people to serve _____.
"He (Asa commanded Judah to seek the Lord God of their fathers and to do the law and the commandment" (II Chron. 14:4).

c. Asa _____ the nation. *"He (Asa) built fortified cities in Judah, for the land had rest; he had no war in those years"* (II Chron. 14:6). *"And Asa had an army of three hundred thousand from Judah…and from Benjamin two hundred and eighty thousand men"* (II Chron. 14:8).

d. Asa relied on the Lord to _____.
When attacked, *"Asa cried out to the Lord his God, and said, 'Lord, it is nothing for You to help, whether with many or with those who have no power; help us, O Lord our God, for we rest on You, and in Your name we go against this multitude. O Lord, You are our God; do not let man prevail against You!"* (II Chron. 14:11).

4. Asa led the nation in revival (II Chronicles 15:1-19).

a. Had the people _____. *"For a longtime Israel has been without the true God, without teaching priest, without law"* (II Chron. 15:3).

b. Reinstituted _____.
"Restored the altar of the Lord that was before the vestibule of the Lord" (II Chron. 15:8).

   c. Celebrated the _____.
      "They gathered together at Jerusalem…and they offered to the Lord" (II Chron. 15:10-11).

   d. Led the people in _____.
      "They entered into the covenant to seek the Lord God of their fathers with all their heart and with all their soul" (II Chron. 15:12).

   e. Actually took _____.
      "Then they took an oath before the Lord with a loud voice, with shouting, and trumpets, and ram's horn" (II Chron. 15:14).

C. LESSONS TO TAKE AWAY

1. Sometimes the sinful excesses in parents and grand-parents produce an _____ in children. Notice the conditions when Asa was a child; *"There was no peace to the one who went out…but great turmoil…nation was destroyed by nation, and city by city"* (II Chron. 15:5-6).

2. Sometimes the evil influence of parents produces children _____ than themselves, i.e., Maachah was more evil than Absalom.

3. Be sure your sin will _____. Maachah's sin was known and dealt with.

4. Cursed to the _____. God had promised, *"The Lord thy God is a jealous God, visiting the iniquity of the fathers upon the children to the third and fourth generation of them that hate me"* (Ex. 20:5).
   Absalom → Maachah → Abijam → Asa

5. God _____ raises up righteous children.

6. Sometimes a grandchild has to _____ of a grandparent.

7. A grandchild can become more godly as he/she grows older, i.e., Asa began with _____ , but eventually brought in a _____ .

Lois

A GRANDMOTHER OVERCOMING OBSTACLES

A. LOIS: LIVING BEYOND HER CIRCUMSTANCES

1. Married a _____ just as her daughter Eunice. "Timothy, the son of a certain Jewish woman (Eunice) who believed, but his father was a Greek" (Acts 16:1).

2. What was her life in Lystra?

    a. Not enough Jewish families for a _____.

    b. Not any _____ advantage.

    c. Not many _____ citizens.

3. Lois expected a son but got a _____. "Thy grandmother Lois, and thy mother Eunice" (II Tim. 1:3).

4. Lois became a _____ believer. Paul said, *I call to remembrance the unfeigned faith that is in you (Timothy), which dwelt first in your grandmother Lois"* (II Tim. 1:5). Unfeigned means genuine, not a play actor repeating lines.

5. Lois and Eunice _____ into Timothy. "Continue in the things which you (Timothy) have been assured, knowing for whom you have learned them" (II Tim. 3:14).

   a. The word "whom" is plural, _____.

   b. The word "knowing" is *oida*, i.e., innate knowledge. Their teaching becomes more than knowledge, it became _____.

   c. The word "continue" means the women laid a _____ on which Paul and Timothy built.

6. Lois and Eunice began _____.
   "That from childhood you have known the Holy Scriptures, which are able to make you wise for salvation" (II Tim. 3:15).

   a. The word "childhood" is *brephos*, which means embryo or newborn baby.

   b. The word "known" is *oida*, i.e., innate knowledge.

   c. Holy Scriptures is *braphe*, i.e., writings, which is plural _____ of the Word of God.

   d. "Make you wise into" Greek suggests, "motion into." The women were _____ Timothy into salvation.

7. The women prepared the _____ for Timothy's conversion. *"When I (Paul) call to remembrance the unfeigned faith that is in you, which dwelt first in your grandmother Lois and your mother Eunice, and I am persuaded is in you also"* (II Tim. 1:5).

B. PAUL BUILT ON LOIS AND EUNICE

1. The women _____ on Paul's first
   trip. (Acts 14:6-23). Paul returned on his second trip.
   "Then he came to Derbe and Lystra, and behold a cer-
   tain disciple was there, named Timothy, the son of a cer-
   tain Jewish woman who believed, but his father was a
   Greek" (Acts 16:1). "Believed" is past tense.

2. Timothy _____ under Paul's ministry.
   "To Timothy, my true son in the faith" (I Tim. 1:2). *"To*
   Timothy my beloved son" (II Tim. 1:2).

3. Timothy believed _____.
   "The Jews…stoned Paul and dragged him out of the
   city (Lystra) supposing him to be dead" (Acts 14:19).
   Timothy was probably an eyewitness. *"You have fully*
   known my doctrine, manner of life…persecutions, afflic-
   tions, which came upon me at Antioch, at Iconium, at
   Lystra" (II Tim. 3:10-11).

4. Timothy was _____ by the church
   leaders at Lystra. *"Do not neglect the gift that is in*
   you…with the laying on of hands of the presbytery"
   (I Tim. 4:14). They would have endorsed the training
   given by Lois and Eunice.

5. Timothy was _____ by Paul.
   "Stir up the gift of God which is in you through the lay-
   ing on of my hands" (II Tim. 1:6).

C. LESSONS TO TAKE AWAY

1. When a grandmother has many limitations, she can be a great influence for God _____.

2. Godly children are not automatically raised. It takes:

    a. _____ instruction

    b. _____ instruction

    c. _____ instruction

    d. _____ instruction

    (Adapted from John Wesley)

3. Your home can be a great godly influence, even when a church is not _____.

4. Every grandmother should get the help of a _____ to influence her grandchildren.

5. Giving attention to _____ in a child's education will influence his/her total life.

6. When grandparents can't be all they want to be in life, at least they can be faithful in what's

    _____.

Unknown Grandsons

A. THREE GENERATIONS DOWN

1. From rags to riches to rags in three generations.

    a. Grandfather: poor but _____.

    b. Son: enjoyed riches, but _____.

    c. Grandson: lazy and _____.

2. From sin to salvation to sin in three generations.

    a. Grandfather: wicked but gloriously _____.

    b. Son: enjoyed Christianity but _____.

    c. Grandson: enticed by sin, then _____.

3. From slavery to the Lord to slavery in three generations.

    a. Grandfather Caleb: Slave but _____.

    b. Son-in-law Othniel: Attacked but _____.

    c. Unknown grandson: Loved sin, then a

    _____.

4. The compromising unknown grandsons: what they forgot, what they changed, what they lost.

"And the people served the Lord all the days of Joshua (and Caleb), *and all they days of the elders* (and Othniel) *that outlived Joshua...there was another generation after them that knew not the Lord...they*

*did evil in the sight of the Lord, and served Baalim...
and the anger of the Lord was against them and he
delivered them into the hands of the nations round
about them"* (Judges 2:7-13, ELT).

B. WHAT THEY FORGOT

1. They forgot they had been slaves that _____.

2. They forgot God guided them through the

    _____.

3. They forgot God gave them the _____.

C. WHAT THEY CHANGED

1. They changed their God for _____.

2. They changed their opinion about themselves. They
    no longer saw themselves as delivered slaves, but
    as _____.

3. They changed their _____.
    They no longer separated from the enemy, but took
    them as house-servants, then intermarried with them.

D. WHAT THEY LOST

1. They lost their _____.
    "They did not drive them out" (Judges 1:32).

2. They lost their _____.
    "They forsook the Lord and served Baal" (Judges 2:13).

3. They lost their desire for _____.
   "They turned quickly from the way in which their fathers walked" (Judges 2:17).

E. FIRST GENERATION: CALEB

1. Knew God had _____ from slavery in Egypt.

2. Knew God _____ from Egypt through the Red Sea.

3. Knew God _____ his possessions.
   "Therefore, give me this mountain, whereof the Lord spoke in that day" (Joshua 14:12). *"But my servant Caleb…hath followed me fully, him will I bring into the land to possess it"* (Num. 14:24).

F. SECOND GENERATION: OTHNIEL

"And he (Caleb) gave him (Othniel) Achsah his daughter to wife" (Joshua 15:17). *"The children of Israel served Chu-shan-rish-a-tha-im eight years. When the children of Israel cried…the Lord raised up a deliver…Othniel"* (Judges 3:8-9).

1. Othniel's generation lost their _____.
   "The children of Israel dwelt among the Canaanites" (Judges 3:5).

2. Othniel's generation lost their _____.
   "Forgot the Lord their God" (Judges 3:7).

3. Othniel's generation lost their _____.
   "Took their daughters to be their wives" (Judges 3:6).

G. WHAT THE THIRD GENERATION: GRANDSONS MUST DO

1. Must be wise to _____.
   "The Lord left to prove Israel...even as many as had not known the wars of Canaan" (Judges 3:3-5, ELT).

2. Must be strong to _____.
   "These nations...the Lord allows to stay...to teach Israel to fight" (Judges 3:1, ELT).

3. Must have conviction to _____.
   "They were to prove Israel...to know whether they (Israel) *would harken unto the commandments of the Lord"* (Judges 3:4).

Joash

A Good Grandson Comes from an Evil Grandmother

A. INTRODUCTION

1. _____ "
   Visiting the iniquity of the fathers (or mothers) upon the children unto the third and fourth generation of them that hate me" (Ex. 20:5).

NORTH	SOUTH
Ahab and Jezebel	Jehoshaphat
↓	↓
Athaliah married	Jehoram
	Ahaziah
	Athaliah
	Joash

2. _____: Great grandmother Jezebel was the power behind the throne of Ahab.

   a. Built _____ to Baal – I Kings 18:19

   b. Hired _____ for Baal – I Kings 18:22

29

    c. _____ godly priest who opposed her – I Kings 18:4

    d. _____ Elijah – I Kings 19:3

    e. _____ Naboth – I Kings 21:1-16

3. _____ : Grandmother Athaliah was a "chippette off thee olde block." Athaliah was as mean as Jezebel her mother.

    a. _____ the throne when her son Ahaziah died.

    b. _____ all her grandsons (no threat to her reign) (II Kings 11:2).

    c. _____ over power – II Kings 11:14.

B. WHY THE GRANDSON TURNED OUT GOOD

1. The influence of a _____ .
His great aunt Jehosheba (the sister of Athaliah) hid (saved) Joash from slaughter. *"Took Joash the son of Ahaziah, and stole him from the king's sons which were slain, and they hid him, even him and his nurse, in the bedchamber from Athaliah, so that he was not slain"* (II Kings 11:2).

2. The influence of a _____ .
Joash was raised in the temple. *"He (Joash) was with them, hid in the house of God six years and Athaliah reigned over the land"* (II Chron. 22:12).

3. The influence of a _____. The high
   priest Jehoiada was the godly_____ influence in Joash's life.

   a. Jehoiada _____. *"He said unto them
      Behold the king's son shall reign; as the Lord hath
      said of the sons of David"* (II Chron. 23:3).

   b. Jehoiada _____. *"So the Levites and
      Judah did according to all things which Jehoiada the
      priest commanded"* (23:8).

4. A _____ coronation. *"And they
   brought out the king's son, put the crown on him, gave
   him the testimony, and made him king. Then Jehoiada
   and his sons anointed him, and said, 'Long live the
   king!'"* (II Chron. 23:11).

5. The _____ of God.
   *"Yet the Lord would not destroy the house of David, be-
   cause of the covenant that He had made with David,
   and since He had promised to give a lamp to him and to
   his sons forever"* (II Chron. 21:7).

   a. Joash was the _____ of David left.

   b. This was Satan's attempt to _____.

C. A GOOD GRANDSON

1. _____.
   *"Then Jehoiada made a covenant between himself, the
   people, and the king, that they should be the Lord's people"* (II Chron. 23:16).

2. _____. *"And
   all the people went to the temple of Baal, and tore*

it down. They broke in pieces its altars and images,
and killed Mattan the priest of Baal before the altars"
(II Chron. 23:17).

3. _____. *"Also*
Jehoiada appointed the oversight of the house of the Lord
to the hand of the priests, the Levites, whom David had
assigned in the house of the Lord, to offer the burnt of-
ferings of the Lord, as it is written in the Law of Moses,
with rejoicing and with singing, as it was established by
David" (II Chron. 23:18).

4. _____. *"And he set*
the gatekeepers at the gates of the house of the Lord, so
that no one who was in any way unclean should enter"
(II Chron. 23:19).

5. _____. *"They came*
through the high gate into the king's house, and set him
upon the throne of the kingdom" (II Chron. 23:20).

6. _____. *"Joash did*
what was right in the sight of the Lord all the days of
Jehoiada the priest" (II Chron. 24:2).

D. HOW TO RAISE GODLY GRANDCHILDREN

1. Make sure they are protected from the
_____. A godly relative can
_____ the influence of an un-
godly relative.

2. Raise them in the _____ of a good
home, Sunday school, AWANA, etc.

3. All the _____ of a church are needed to help influence a child for godliness.

4. _____ the significant "passages" of life in a godly way.

5. _____ of evil forces from a child's life.

6. Make sure children make _____ and use your influence to keep them from making bad decisions.

7. When a child doesn't have discipline, give him an environment where they do the right thing and they can develop _____.

Mephibosheth

Living Below
your Inheritance

A. REASONS SOME LIVE BELOW THEIR INHERITANCE

1. _____. The grandson was not strong as his father and grandfather. *"Jonathan...had a son that was lame in his feet. He was five years old when the tidings came (of grandfather and father's death) and his nurse took him up and fled: and it came to pass and she made hast to flee, that she fell, and he became lame"* (II Sam. 2:2).

   a. An _____.

   b. Not one foot, but _____.

   c. Kept the boy from physical _____.

   d. Kept the boy from growing _____.

   e. Negative _____.

2. _____. The name Mephibosheth means, "Shame that destroys."

3. _____. His grandfather Saul disobeyed God, tried to kill David, and visited a

witch. His father Jonathan was godly, but died with Saul under the judgment of God (I Sam. 28:18-19).

4. _____. He was living out of the Promised Land, east across Jordan in Lodebar (means no pasture).

5. _____. He was being taken care of by Machir. No home, no money, and no way to make a living.

B. LIVING LESS THAN CHRISTIAN

1. _____. *"Made us alive together with Christ…raised us up together, and made us sit together in heavenly places in Christ Jesus"* (Eph. 2:5-6).

2. _____. Jesus Christ has blessed us with every spiritual blessing in the heavenly places in Christ" (Eph. 1:3).

3. _____. *"For the good that I will do, I do not do, and the evil that I will not do, that I practice"* (Rom. 7:19).

4. _____. *"Thanks be unto God who always leads up in triumph in Christ"* (II Cor. 2:14).

C. WHY THE GRANDSON WAS ELEVATED

1. _____. *"David said, 'is there yet any that is left in the house of Saul, that I*

may show him kindness for Jonathan's sake'" (II Sam. 9:1).

    a.   Jonathan gave up his "rights" for David. Jesus gave up his "right" for us. *"Christ Jesus...being in the form of God...taking the form of a servant, and coming in the likeness of man"* (Phil. 2:5-7).

    b.   _____, and the acid test of your character.

2.   _____. Mephibosheth would have been forgotten except a servant remembered. *"And Ziba said unto the king, 'Jonathan hath yet a son'"* (II Sam. 9:3).

3.   _____. David didn't do this for himself or his reputation. *"That I may show the kindness of God to him"* (II Sam. 9:3).

D. HOW TO BE ELEVATED

1.   _____. *"And he (Mephibosheth) answered, 'Behold your servant'"* (II Sam. 7:6).

2.   _____. *"And he bowed himself and said...that thou shouldest look upon a dead dog"* (II Sam. 9:8).

3.   _____. "The king said...I have given you...all that pertaineth to Saul and to all his house" (II Sam. 9:9).

    a.   _____. *"If then you were raised with Christ, seek those things which are above"* (Col. 3:1).

b. _____. *"Set your aim on things above, not on things on this earth"* (Col. 3:2).

If God has given us all spiritual things, why are we living with only a few things?

---

4. _____. *Mephibosheth didn't have another worry about food, "But Mephibosheth… shall eat at my table"* (II Sam. 9:11).

   a. _____. *"My God shall supply all your needs"* (Phil. 4:19).

   b. _____. *"Delight yourself also in the Lord, and He shall give you the desire of your heart"* (Psa. 37:4).

5. _____. *"You Ziba and your sons and your servants shall work the land for Mephibosheth to bring in the harvest that Mephibosheth's sons will have to eat"* (II Sam. 9:10).

   a. The _____. *"And I will pray the father, and he will give you another helper"* (John 14:16).

   b. _____. We have the "communion of saints."

6. _____. *"Mephibosheth dwelt in Jerusalem for he ate continually at the kings table and he was lame in both feet"* (II Sam. 9:13).

   a. Daily _____. *"That I may dwell in the house of the Lord forever"* (Psa. 23:6).

b. Daily _____. *"That I may dwell in the house of the Lord all the days of my life, to behold the beauty of the Lord"* (Psa. 27:4).

E. TO TAKE AWAY

1. You may lose your _____ with God, but you can never lose your _____ to God.

   a. You will always have your forefather's blood in your veins.

   b. A _____ son is still a son.

2. Your forefathers _____ more than you realize.

3. You must change your _____ about your forefathers to enjoy their benefits.

4. You must _____ the benefits that are yours.

5. You can _____ lost fellowship with forefathers.

6. You can benefit from your forefathers, even.

Samuel

When Grandchildren are Pushed into Ministry

"Now it came to pass when Samuel was old that he made his sons judges over Israel. The name of his first-born was Joel, and the name of his second, Abijah; they were judges in Beersheba. But his sons did not walk in his ways; they turned aside after dishonest gain, took bribes, and perverted justice. Then all the elders of Israel gathered together and came to Samuel at Ramah, and said to him, "Look, you are old, and your sons do not walk in your ways. Now make us a king to judge us like all the nations" (I Sam. 8:1-5).

---

1. Three generations: Hannah → Samuel → Joel and Abijah.

2. God _____. *"The Lord raised up judges which delivered them"* (Judges 2:16). Samuel made his sons judges.

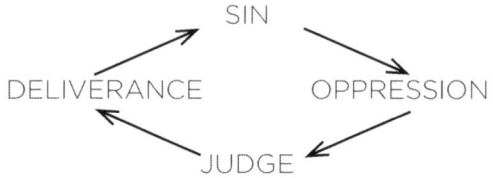

3. Joel and Abijah were not _____. "When Samuel was old (age 60) he made his sons judges over Israel" (I Sam. 8:1).

4. Why Samuel may be right to appoint sons.

   a. _____. It was not a time of war.

   b. _____. God used fathers in the past to put their sons into office.

   c. _____. Samuel did for sons what his mother Hannah did for him.

5. Why Samuel may have been wrong.

   a. _____. Samuel missed God's leading, he would live 38 more years.

   b. Samuel forgot the _____. The high priest before Samuel did not properly correct his sons. *"I (God) have warned him (Eli) continually…because his sons are blaspheming God; and he has not disciplined them"* (I Sam. 3:13, NLB).

   c. Their _____. The sons were in ministry for the wrong reasons. *"His (Samuel) sons walked not in his ways"* (I Sam. 8:3).

   d. _____. *"The elders… said unto him (Samuel)…thy sons walk not in thy ways"* (I Sam. 8:4-5).

a. _____. "The thing displeased Samuel when they said give us a king to judge us" (I Sam. 8:6).

b. _____. Prematurely instituted a (wrong) king, i.e., Saul. "The elders said...make us a king to judge us all the nations" (I Sam. 8:4, 6).

B. THE SON'S GODLY HERITAGE

1. Grandmother Hannah's godly walk.

   a. Believed in _____. *"She (Hannah) wept and did not eat...prayed unto the Lord, and wept"* (I Sam. 1:7, 10).

   b. Was _____. *"Out of the abundance of my complaint and grief have I spoken hitherto"* (I Sam. 1:16).

   c. _____. *"Now I am giving him (Samuel) to the Lord, and he will belong to the Lord his whole life"* (I Sam. 1:28, NLB).

   d. _____. *"Then Hannah prayed, my heart rejoices in the Lord"* (I Sam. 2:1).

2. Samuel faithfully served.

   a. _____. *"The child Samuel ministered unto the Lord"* (I Sam.3:1).

   b. _____. *"The Lord said to Samuel"* (I Sam. 3:11).

   c. _____. *"Samuel judged Israel all the days of his life"* (I Sam. 7:15).

3. What the sons did wrong.

   a. _____. *"His* (Samuel)
      sons walked not in his ways" (I Sam. 8:3).

   b. _____. The sons
      "turned aside for lucre" (v.3).

   c. _____. The sons
      "took bribes" (v.3).

   d. _____. The sons
      "perverted judgment" (v.3).

When money is your primary goal, You
will eventually break some law.

C. HOW TO TRAIN CHILDREN ABOUT MONEY

1. Teach them _____. Stewardship
   is the proper management of time, talent and treasure
   for the glory of God. *"Moreover, stewards must faith-*
   fully manage every thing for God" (I Cor. 4:2, ELT).

2. Teach them that _____.
   "False teachers think…financial gain is godliness"
   (I Tim. 6:3, 5, ELT). *"Godliness that is satisfied with*
   what God gives is great gain" (I Tim. 6:6, ELT).

3. Teach them that lust for money will _____.
   "The love of money is at the root of all kinds of evil,
   and some people craving money have wandered from
   the faith, and pierced themselves with many sorrows"
   (I Tim. 6:10).

4. Teach them _____. *"But thou O man of God, flee these things (lust of money), and follow after righteousness, godliness, faith, love, patience and meekness"* (I Tim. 6:11).

5. Teach them to _____.
"He that had received one (talent), went and digged in the earth and hid his lord's money" (Matthew 25:18).

Grandpa Mordecai

Being an Unobserved Influence

Grandpa Mordecai—Influential through _____.

   Esther—Influential through _____,

Grandson Artaxerxes—Influential for _____.

"There was a certain Jew whose name was Mordecai the son of...Kish, a Benjamite. And Mordecai had brought up Hadassah, that is, Esther, his uncle's daughter, for she had neither father nor mother. The young woman was lovely and beautiful. When her father and mother died, Mordecai took her as his own daughter" (Esther 2:5,7).

A. WHAT IS KNOWN ABOUT THE FAMILY

1. _____. What was Mordecai's background? *"A Jew...named Mordecai,...the Son of Kish* (Saul) *a Benjamite"* (Est. 2:5).

2. _____. What is known about Esther's home? *"Her father and mother were dead"* (Est. 2:7).

3. _____. Who raised Esther? *"He (Mordecai) brought up Hadassah, that is Esther, his uncle's daughter…took her for his own daughter"* (Est. 2:7). Esther and Mordecai were cousins.

4. _____. What was known about Esther? *"Esther was fair and beautiful"* (Est. 2:7). Her inner character enhanced her outer beauty. She won the beauty contest to become the next queen.

5. God works His influence when His people can't outwardly testify.

   a. Jewish name Myrtle, _____.

   b. Gentle name star, _____.

   c. To win contest. *"Esther had not revealed her people or kindred"* (Est. 2:10).

6. What was Esther's contribution?

   a. Her _____ stopped wicked Haman.

   b. Her _____ gave the Jews a way to defend themselves.

   c. She was the wife to the most _____.

   d. Her son (Artaxerxes) used his influence to rebuild Jerusalem's walls (i.e., set up the city-state again).

7. Principles

   a. God can greatly use _____.

   b. Those who adopt _____ through their children.

c. What you are – _____ – is more important than family heritage or outward physical appearance.

d. You don't have to be a tinkling bell to be

_____.

B. INFLUENCE BY THE GRANDSON ARTAXERXES

Grandfather Mordecai—by _____.

Mother Esther—double royalty (_____).

_____ Father Ahasurus— also named Xerxes.

Grandson Artaxerxes—Arta means "_____."

1. _____. If Artaxerxes is the son of Esther and Xerxes, why is it not clear in secular history? A historian said it will "probably remain forever a mystery."

2. If everyone knew everything God was doing, they would try to become a Christian _____.

3. Why would Artaxerxes choose Nehemiah?

a. Jewish cupbearer.

b. Trusted _____ (physically big).

4. _____. What was Nehemiah's passion? *The wall of Jerusalem is broken down…the gates are burned"* (Neh. 1:3). *"When I heard these words, I sat and wept and mourned many days"* (Neh. 1:4).

5. _____. How did Artaxerxes, hear of Jerusalem's problems? "I had never been sad in the kings presence before." Therefore the king said, 'Why is your face sad?'" (Neh. 2:1-2).

6. _____. What did Nehemiah do at the moment of spiritual crisis? *"So I prayed to the God of Heaven"* (Neh. 2:4).

7. _____. This request was ill-timed in light of secular history's record of battles with Egypt, Greece, Cypress, and a general who led an insurrection.

8. Why was Artaxerxes' permission to re-build Jerusalem so "unusual?"

   a. Jews had a history of being _____.

   b. Small nations around Jerusalem _____.

   c. Kingdom in _____.

   d. Yet God works behind the scenes.

9. How did Artaxerxes help rebuild Jerusalem?

   a. A letter of _____. *"I (Nehemiah) said to the king…let letters be given to me for the governors of the region"* (Neh. 2:7).

   b. _____. *"A letter to Asaph…give me timber"* (Neh. 2:8).

10. How influential was Artaxerxes in God's eternal plan?

    a. _____. The Jews had returned from captivity in 536 A.D. and 516 A.D. and set up worship, then rebuilt the temple, but did not have a central seat of authority.

a. _____. The Jews in the Promised Land needed a city for protection from bands of outlaws and marauding armies. They needed national self respect.

b. _____. *"From the command (454 BC) to restore and build Jerusalem until Messiah the Prince, there shall be seven weeks, and sixty-two weeks; the street shall be built again, and the wall, even in troublesome times. And after sixty-two weeks shall Messiah be cut off* (30 A.D.)"* (Daniel 9:25-26).

C. PRINCIPLES

1. Just as Grandpa Mordecai used his _____ for God, so did Artaxerxes. Good children are influenced by the way their parents influenced them.

2. You can be influential for God when you are in a setting where you cannot be _____.

3. God causes great events to happen in _____.

4. When your world is blackest, a _____.

Moses

Grandfather—Moses— _____.

Father—Gershom— _____.

Good son—Jonathan— _____.

"Then the children of Dan set up for themselves the carved image; and Jonathan the son of Gershom, the son of Moses, and his sons were priests to the tribe of Dan until the day of the captivity of the land" (Judges 18:30).

A. THE GRANDFATHER MOSES

1. The accomplishments of Moses.

    a. _____. What Moses did?
        "And by means of many miraculous signs, and wonders, he led them out of Egypt, through the Red Sea, and back and forth through the wilderness for forty years" (Acts 7:36, NLB).

    b. _____. What Moses said.
        "Moses was learned in all the wisdom of the Egyptians, and was mighty in word" (Acts 7:22).

c. _____. Who Moses was. *"Moses was very meek, above all the men which were upon the face of the earth"* (Num. 12:3).

d. The _____. How is Moses characterized?

e. _____. What was Moses' most influential accomplishment? *"Now it came to pass, when Moses had finished setting up the Tabernacle, that he anointed it and consecrated it and all its furnishings, and the altar and all its utensils; so he anointed them and consecrated them"* (Num. 7:1).

2. Gershom: A famous father and an infamous son.

a. _____. Who was Gershom? *"She (Zipporah) bore him a son, and he (Moses) called his name Gershom, for he said, 'I have been a stranger in a strange land'"* (Ex. 2:22).

b. The sons of famous men are not usually _____.

B. JONATHAN: A GRANDSON'S FALL FROM GREATNESS

1. Jonathan was given a spiritual direction in life, but he didn't follow it. His name means _____.

2. Jonathan wanted, to be famous like his grandfather Moses, but apart from Moses _____.

a. Jonathan sold out for _____. *"Micah said...I will give thee ten shekels of silver"* (Judges 17:10).

b. Jonathan wanted _____. *"Micah said…I will give thee…a suit of apparel and thy victuals"* (Judges 17:10).

3. Jonathan wanted to serve the Lord like his grandfather Moses, but was not _____.

a. Moses was "called" by God at the burning bush, but Jonathan was "called" by _____ named Micah. *"Micah consecrated the Levite (Jonathan)"* (Judges 18:12).

b. Jonathan yielded to _____. *"Six hundred warriors from the tribe of Dan stood outside the gates…they said…'Come with us'"* (Judges 18:16, 19, NLB). Those who serve the Lord for money, willingly change jobs when a better offer comes along. Jonathan's response "His heart was glad" (Judges 18:20).

c. Jonathan wanted the vast influence of his grandfather Moses, but yielded to the _____. *"The men of Dan said, 'Isn't it better to be a priest for an entire tribe of Israel, than just for the household of one man?'"* (Judges 18:19).

d. Jonathan wanted the supernatural power of his grandfather Moses, but was treated as a _____. *"Now know I the Lord will bless me, seeing I have hired a Levite as my priest"* (Judges 17:13, ELT).

C. JONATHAN'S SIN

1. Incomplete _____. He didn't
   worship at Shiloh. *"In Shiloh before the Lord at the
   door of the Tabernacle"* (Joshua 19:31).

When a beginning preacher
gets away from the church
he is heading for trouble.

---

2. Obvious _____. He worshipped
   graven images. *"Thou shalt not make unto thee any
   graven images...thou shalt not bow down, nor serve
   them, for I the Lord thy God I am a jealous God, visiting the iniquity of the fathers upon the children unto the
   third and fourth generations"* (Ex. 20:4-5).

3. Flagrant _____. He created
   a separate house of worship. *"All the time the house of
   God was in Shiloh"* (18:31).

4. Arrogantly _____. He falsely
   claimed to speak for God. Jonathan told the Danites,
   *"Go in peace, may the presence of the Lord be with you
   on your way"* (Judges 18:6). But the Danites slaugh-
   tered, stole, and took hostages.

5. Perplexing _____. How could
   Jonathan begin so high, yet fall into heresy and apos-
   tasy? He forgot his grandfather's first law, *"Thou shalt
   love the Lord thy God with all thy heart, with all thy
   soul, and with all thy might"* (Deut. 6:5).

D. HELPING A DOCTRINAL PRODIGAL

1. _____. *"Again I say to you that if two of you agree on earth concerning anything that they ask, it will be done for them by My Father in Heaven"* (Matt. 18:19).

2. Be _____ in their life. *"Brethren, if anyone among you wanders from the truth, and someone turns him back, let him know that he who turns a sinner from the error of his way will save a soul from death and cover a multitude of sins"* (James 5:19-20).

3. Point out _____. *"He who knows God, hears us; he who is not of God does not hear us. By this we know the spirit of truth and the spirit of error"* (I John 4:6).

4. Quietly _____ (don't argue). *"Aquila and Priscilla...took him (Apollos) aside and explained to him the way of God more accurately"* (Acts 18:26).

5. Their reason to sin is usually not their _____. *"The love of money is a root of all kinds of evil for which some have strayed from the faith in their greediness"* (I Tim. 6:10).

6. Always _____. *"But when he (the prodigal son) was still a great way off, his father saw him, and had compassion, and ran and fell on his neck and kissed him"* (Luke 15:20).

Noah

Grandfather—Noah—_____.
Father—Ham—Gossiped.
Grandson—Canaan—_____.

"And Noah began to be a farmer, and he planted a vineyard. Then he drank of the wine and was drunk, and became uncovered in his tent. And Ham, the father of Canaan, saw the nakedness of his father, and told his two brothers outside. But Shem and Japheth took a garment, laid it on both their shoulders, and went backward and covered the nakedness of their father. Their faces were turned away, and they did not see their father's nakedness. So Noah awoke from his wine, and knew what his younger son had done to him. Then he said: 'Cursed be Canaan; a servant of servants He shall be to his brethren'" (Gen. 9:20-25).

A. WHAT WE KNOW FOR SURE

1. _____. What is known about Noah? *"Noah was a just man and perfect…and Noah walked with God"* (Gen. 6:9).

2. _____. Why did Noah build an ark? *"By faith Noah being divinely warned of things not yet seen moved with godly fear, prepared an ark...by which he condemned the world"* (Heb. 11:7).

3. _____. What was Noah's occupation? *"God said to Noah...make yourself an ark of gopher wood"* (Gen. 6:14).

4. _____. How did Noah warn the world? *"Noah...a preacher of righteousness"* (II Peter 2:5).

5. _____. What sins did Jesus mention Noah preached against? *"As the days of Noah were, so also will be the coming of the Son of Man...drinking...until the day Noah entered the ark"* (Matt. 24:37-38).

6. _____. What were other sins the people committed? (Gen. 6:1-13).

7. _____. When did Noah enter the ark? *"The Lord said to Noah, 'Come thou and all thy house into the ark'"* (Gen. 7:1). He was 600 years old (see Gen. 8:13).

8. _____. What was Noah's new occupation after the flood? *"Noah began to be a husbandman, and planted a vineyard"* (9:20).

9. What was Noah's threefold sin? *"He (Noah) drank of the wine, and was drunken, and he was uncovered within the tent"* (Gen. 9:21).

   a. _____. He preached against it.

b. _____. He uncovered himself, i.e.,
   gulah (reflective)

c. _____.

10. How did Noah know? *"Noah awoke from his wine,
    and knew what his younger son had done to him"* (9:24).

a. Special _____.

b. _____. He asked or was told.

c. _____. A drunk man remembers
   some things.

B. WHAT WAS THE SIN OF HAM AND CANAAN?

1. _____. *"Ham, the father
   of Canaan saw the nakedness of his father, and told his
   two brethren"* (Gen. 9:22). What went with seeing?

a. _____.

b. _____.

c. _____ of father's authority to His
   God. (Morris)

d. _____, i.e., showing disrespect.

2. _____. *"Shem and Japheth took a gar-
   ment, and laid it upon their shoulders, and went backward, and covered the nakedness of their father;...and
   saw not their father's nakedness"* (Gen. 9:23).

3. Why curse Canaan?

a. _____. Ham was the youngest
   son of Noah, and Canaan youngest son of Ham
   (Gen. 10:6).

b. _____. This was not a "angry" grandfather. Since only God could know the future, Noah spoke by God's revelation. God cursed Canaan for what he did, and what He was to become.

c. Noah recognized a _____. Noah/God saw a weakness in Canaan and knew it would be perpetuated.

d. _____ always suffers the most, *"cursed be Canaan, a servant of servants, shall he be to his brethren"* (Gen. 9:25).

1. When was the curse carried out?

   a. The Canaanites become a _____. God describes them *"uncovered the nakedness"* (Lev. 18:3).

   b. The curse was carried out when Joshua and Israel _____ the Canaanites (see Joshua 11,12).

C. WHAT LESSONS CAN BE LEARNED ABOUT SINNING GRANDPARENTS

1. You never get _____.

2. You can fall at your _____. *"Let him that thinketh he standeth take heed lest he fall"* (I Cor. 10:12).

3. Your fall can hurt _____. *"Cursed be Canaan."*

4. Your fall can come after God has _____.
   Noah, Elijah, Peter, Paul, Uriah, David.

5. Just because you have done a lot for God, doesn't
   mean He will_____ _____.

6. The careless root of sin in a grandfather or father (lust
   or rebellion) can have _____ in grandchildren.

7. Drunkenness is not a _____, nor is
   it something God overlooks.

8. The body is the temple of the Holy Spirit, and the
   child of God should be modest.

   a. Applies to _____.
   b. Applies to _____.
   c. Applies to _____.

9. Hitherto repressed _____ will surface
   when given the opportunity.

D. WHAT GRANDPARENTS AND GRANDCHILDREN NEED TO KNOW

1. God _____. *"No temptation
   has overtaken you except such as is common to man; but
   God is faithful, who will not allow you to be tempted be-
   yond what you are able, but with the temptation will also make the way of escape, that you may be able to bear
   it"* (I Cor. 10:13).

2. God _____. *"He who commits
   sexual immorality, sins against his own body. Do you
   not know that your body is the temple of the Holy Spirit,
   who is in you…you are not your own"* (I Cor. 6:18-19).

3. Old age sin _____. *"But I discipline my body and bring it into subjection, lest, when I have preached to others, I myself should become disqualified"* (I Cor. 9:27).

Paul a Spiritual Grandfather

A Disciple-making Grandparent

"And the things that you have heard from me among many witnesses, commit these to faithful men who will be able to teach others also" (II Tim. 2:2).

Spiritual Grandfather—Paul—_____.

Son in ministry—Timothy—_____.

Third Generation—Faithful men—_____.

Fourth Generation—Others—_____.

A. WHAT GRANDPARENTS DO THAT PARENTS DON'T DO

1. Grandparents make you feel _____, while parents treat you as _____.

2. Grandparents can deal with _____, while parents must deal with _____.

3. Grandparents point out your _____, while parents must deal with your _____.

4. Grandparents can _____, while parents must deal with your personal _____.

5. Grandparents have learned what is _____, and can overlook _____.

B. WHAT IS A DISCIPLE-MAKING GRANDPARENT?

1. 1. You are a reproducer of _____.

    a. Because children are _____ they _____ your examples.

    b. How you _____ is how they will be grandparents for future generations.

    _____.

    _____.

    _____.

    _____.

2. Your life will outlive your _____.

3. You pour _____ into them. *"As apostles of Christ…we were gentle among you as a parent cherishing a baby…giving you not only the gospel, but we poured our own lives into you"* (I Thess. 2:7-8, ELT).

4. You become _____ to them.

5. You have not finished until they pour _____, what you poured into them.

C. WHAT DOES A DISCIPLE LOOK LIKE?

1. Makes a _____ for salvation.
   *"Then He said to them all, 'If anyone desires to come af-
   ter Me, let him deny himself, and take up his cross daily,
   and follow Me'"* (Luke 9:23).

2. Has a dedication to be _____.
   *"Christ...leaving us an example that we should follow
   His steps"* (I Peter 2:21).

3. Learns to _____ in Christ. *"I am
   the Vine, you are the branches. He who abides in Me,
   and I in him, bears much fruit; for without Me you can
   do nothing"* (John 15:5).

4. Learns to live by the _____. *"If you
   abide in My Word, you are My disciples indeed. And you
   shall know the truth, and the truth will make you free"*
   (John 8:31-32).

5. Knows how to _____.
   *"If you abide in Me, and My words abide in you, you
   will ask what you desire, and it shall be done for you"*
   (John 15:7).

6. Makes _____. *"A new command-
   ment I give to you, that you love one another; as I have
   loved you, that you also love one another"* (John 13:34).

7. Testifies to and serves _____.
   *"Greater love has no one than this, than to lay down
   one's life for his friends"* (John 15:13).

D. HOW DISCIPLE-MAKERS DO IT

1. By _____. Paul told Timothy, *"You have carefully followed My doctrine, manner of life, purpose, faith, longsuffering, love, perseverance, persecution…"* (II Tim. 3:10-11).

"Example is not the main thing, it is the only thing"
—Albert Schweitzer

---

2. By _____. Paul called Timothy, *"My beloved son"* (II Tim. 1:2).

3. By _____. Paul sent Timothy to minister in Corinth, Macedonia, Philippi, Thessalonica, etc.

4. By _____. Timothy heard Paul preach publicly and privately, i.e., "heard of me."

5. By _____. The two personal letters are reflections of their private conversations.

6. By _____. Paul listed Timothy's name with his six times. Paul publicly expressed appreciation for Timothy (see I Cor. 4:17), and told the Philippians, *"For I have no one like-minded (like Timothy) who will care for your state"* (Phil. 2:20).

7. By _____. Timothy needed a "jump start." *"Stir up the gift of God which is in you"* (II Tim. 1:6). *"Be strong"* (II Tim. 2:1).

Key:

LESSON 1
Poor
Absentee
Physically weak
Nothing
His testimony
Were like
Receive Christ
Changed
Word of God
Name
Words
Expectations
Wealth
Influence
Nation
Land
Grandmother
Travel
Was there
Almost home
Road
Adopted
Kissed and hugged
His hands on them
Blessed
His name
God's future
His love
Example of worship
Position
Attitude
Spiritual example
Testimony
Naturally

LESSON 2
Spiritual priorities
To the Lord

Family influence
Criticized
Naomi recognized God's punishment
Naomi's counsel toward family heritage
Redemption
Patience and trust
More importance
Identified
Famous in Israel
Great grandfather
Worshipper of God
Servant
Purpose in life
Compromiser
Conviction
Any hope
New life
Spiritual energy
Nourished
The love
Influencing
Second chance
A maid

LESSON 3
Fighter
Rebellious
Murdered
Kill
Compromise
Split
Corrupted
Evil name
Sodomy
False gods
Sexual
Spirit-demon
Evil
Sins
Sovereignly prepared
Outward idolatry
The Lord

Armed and fortified
Defend the nation
Taught the scriptures
Blood sacrifice
Feast to the Lord
Dedication
An oath
Opposite reaction
More evil
Expose you
Third or fourth generation
Sovereignly
Deal with the sins
Reforms
Revival

LESSON 4
Gentile
Synagogue
Civilized
Roman
Daughter
Genuine
Poured their faith
Both taught
His conviction
Foundation
Teaching early
All parts
Moving
Spiritual foundation
Were converted
Believed in Christ
In spite of persecution
Recommended
Ordained
Though your children
Early
Plain
Frequent
Patient
Available to help

Godly role model
Small details
Given them in life

LESSON 5
Worked hard for money
Didn't earn them
Lost all
Transformed from sin
Lived on father's faith
Corrupted by sin
Great character
Survived
Slave
God delivered
Red Sea and the desert
Promised Land
Idols
Satisfied plantation owners
Relationship to sin
Pioneering spirit
Conviction of belief
Separation from sin
Freed him
Led him
Gave him
Pioneering spirit
Beliefs
Separation from sin
Recognize sin
Fight sin
Follow the Lord

LESSON 6
Generational sins
Corrupter
Sanctuary
Priest
Killed
Threatened
Lied and murdered
Ruthless

Seized
Killed
Neurotic
Good woman
Godly environment
Good grand uncle
Believed
Planned
Regal
Sovereignty
Only seed
Cut off Messiah
Joash made a pledge of devotion
Joash cleansed the land of sin
Joash reinstituted worship
Enforced discipline
Joash was loyal to the symbols of office
Good testimony
Evil one
Offset
Godly environment
Resources
Celebrate
Get rid
Good decisions
Self-discipline

LESSON 7
Physical problems
Accident
Both feet
Activity
Physically strong
Self-perception
Name problems
Heritage problems
Geographical problems
Indigent
Ignore our new position
Not enjoy heavenly things
Obsessed with temptation
Defeated

Another's work
Gratitude is the lest remembered of all virtues
God uses people
Right motivation
Realize you are not worthy
Recognize you are dead
Know all things that are yours
Spiritual things
Heavenly goals
Appropriate daily food
Our needs
Our desire
Get help
Holy Spirit
Believers
Enjoy the king's presence
Fellowship
Worship
Fellowship
Relationship
Prodigal
Love you
Thinking
Claim
Restore
After their death

LESSON 8
Raised up judges
Raised up by God
No crisis
God uses human means
Mother's example
Premature
Poor example of Eli
Weak character
People rejected sons
Father reacted
Political results
Prayer and fasting
Singled focused
Dedicated her child to God

Worshipped God
Served faithfully
Talked with God
Did not quit
Rejected Samuel's attitudes and actions
Served for money
Sold out to money
Violated the law
Stewardship
Money gain is not godliness
Destroy them
Christian convictions
Use money properly

LESSON 9
Adoption
Strategy
Israel
Royal blood
Orphaned
Adopted
Attractive
Grows underneath canopy
Can't be seen in sunlight
Strategy
Influence
Powerful king on earth
Adopted children
Can influence the world
Character
Influential for God
Adoption
Birth and marriage
Son
The hidden hand of God
For the wrong reasons
Protection
Jerusalem
His relationship to a Jewish- cupbearer
Pray
Kingdom turmoil
Rebellious

Opposed it
Turmoil
Authority
Money and resources
The walls gave self-government
The walls were a rallying point
The walls started the prophecy- clock ticking
Hidden influence
Outwardly Christian
Seemingly small ways
Hidden star may shine

LESSON 10
Lawgiver
Undistinguished
Prodigal priest
Leadership
Ability
Humble
Deliverer
Set up a place of worship
His name means stranger
Famous themselves
Jehovah has given
Integrity
Money
Security
Called of God
A man
Pressure
Influence of greed
Good luck charm
Obedience
Disobedience
Heresy
Deceptive
Question
Pray
Intentional
Difference
Explain
Root reason

Love them

LESSON 11
Sinned
Laughed
Godly
Warned of judgment
Carpenter
Preacher
Drinking
Satan worship
God called
A farmer
Drunken
Exposure
Lack of role model
Revelation
Inquiry
Memory
Seeing only
Lust
Mockery
Rejection
Not covering
Not seeing
Youngest
Divine curse
Rebellious attitude and perverse lust
Third generation
Lustful people
Too old to quit sinning
Greatest strength
Your family
Greatly used you
Overlook your sin in old age
Disastrous results
Private sin
All ages
Sexual exposure
Sexual viewing, i.e., lust
Lust and sexual fantasies
Provides victory

Lives in your body
Will disqualify you

LESSON 12
Disciple-maker
Learner
Passed lessons on
The proof of Christianity
Grown up
A child
Positive gentleness
Negative consequences
Future greatness
Present shortcomings
Build individual initiative
Responsibility and accountability
Eternally important
Immediate issues
Reproducers
Mimickers
Live out
Influence them
Paul
Timothy
Faithful men
Others
Lessons
Your soul
Necessary
Into others
Radical decision
Like Jesus
Abide
Scriptures
Pray
Love the distinguishing mark of life
Others
Example
Association
Assignment
Instruction
Private counsel

Promotion
Prodding

A complete copy of *Grandparents in the Bible: Great Lessons and Grand Blessings* can be purchased on Amazon.com. To get a full explanation of the Bible stories and applications about Grandparents in the Bible; this textbook will give a sound bases for preaching and teaching on Grandparents.

Students who purchase 10 copies of the completed book, the cost is $10 per book. Please order from:

Elmer Towns

PO Box 2294

Forest, VA 24551

Made in the USA
Columbia, SC
22 July 2017